BATH TIME IS FUN TIME

A ten-minute comedy by
Arthur M. Jolly

www.youthplays.com
info@youthplays.com
424-703-5315

Bath Time is Fun Time © 2011 Arthur M. Jolly
All rights reserved. ISBN 978-1-62088-323-5.

Caution: This play is fully protected under the copyright laws of the United States of America, Canada, the British Commonwealth and all other countries of the copyright union and is subject to royalty for all performances including but not limited to professional, amateur, charity and classroom whether admission is charged or presented free of charge.

Reservation of Rights: This play is the property of the author and all rights for its use are strictly reserved and must be licensed by his representative, YouthPLAYS. This prohibition of unauthorized professional and amateur stage presentations extends also to motion pictures, recitation, lecturing, public reading, radio broadcasting, television, video and the rights of adaptation or translation into non-English languages.

Performance Licensing and Royalty Payments: Amateur and stock performance rights are administered exclusively by YouthPLAYS. No amateur, stock or educational theatre groups or individuals may perform this play without securing authorization and royalty arrangements in advance from YouthPLAYS. Required royalty fees for performing this play are available online at www.YouthPLAYS.com. Royalty fees are subject to change without notice. Required royalties must be paid each time this play is performed and may not be transferred to any other performance entity. All licensing requests and inquiries should be addressed to YouthPLAYS.

Author Credit: All groups or individuals receiving permission to produce this play must give the author(s) credit in any and all advertisements and publicity relating to the production of this play. The author's billing must appear directly below the title on a separate line with no other accompanying written matter. The name of the author(s) must be at least 50% as large as the title of the play. No person or entity may receive larger or more prominent credit than that which is given to the author(s) and the name of the author(s) may not be abbreviated or otherwise altered from the form in which it appears in this Play.

Publisher Attribution: All programs, advertisements, flyers or other printed material must include the following notice:
> Produced by special arrangement with YouthPLAYS (www.youthplays.com).

Prohibition of Unauthorized Copying: Any unauthorized copying of this book or excerpts from this book, whether by photocopying, scanning, video recording or any other means, is strictly prohibited by law. This book may only be copied by licensed productions with the purchase of a photocopy license, or with explicit permission from YouthPLAYS.

Trade Marks, Public Figures & Musical Works: This play may contain references to brand names or public figures. All references are intended only as parody or other legal means of expression. This play may also contain suggestions for the performance of a musical work (either in part or in whole). YouthPLAYS has not obtained performing rights of these works unless explicitly noted. The direction of such works is only a playwright's suggestion, and the play producer should obtain such permissions on their own. The website for the U.S. copyright office is *http://www.copyright.gov*.

COPYRIGHT RULES TO REMEMBER

1. To produce this play, you must receive prior written permission from YouthPLAYS and pay the required royalty.

2. You must pay a royalty each time the play is performed in the presence of audience members outside of the cast and crew. Royalties are due whether or not admission is charged, whether or not the play is presented for profit, for charity or for educational purposes, or whether or not anyone associated with the production is being paid.

3. No changes, including cuts or additions, are permitted to the script without written prior permission from YouthPLAYS.

4. Do not copy this book or any part of it without written permission from YouthPLAYS.

5. Credit to the author and YouthPLAYS is required on all programs and other promotional items associated with this play's performance.

When you pay royalties, you are recognizing the hard work that went into creating the play and making a statement that a play is something of value. We think this is important, and we hope that everyone will do the right thing, thus allowing playwrights to generate income and continue to create wonderful new works for the stage.

> Plays are owned by the playwrights who wrote them. Violating a playwright's copyright is a very serious matter and violates both United States and international copyright law. Infringement is punishable by actual damages and attorneys' fees, statutory damages of up to $150,000 per incident, and even possible criminal sanctions. **Infringement is theft. Don't do it.**

Have a question about copyright? Please contact us by email at info@youthplays.com or by phone at 424-703-5315. When in doubt, please ask.

CAST OF CHARACTERS

RUBBER DUCKIE
SPONGE
WASHCLOTH
SUBMARINE

(RUBBER DUCKIE, SPONGE, WASHCLOTH and SUBMARINE are on the edge of a bathtub.)

RUBBER DUCKIE: I think I'm gonna throw up.

SUBMARINE: You were lucky. I was in it. I mean...in it!

SPONGE: It got into me. I could feel it. It went inside me. *(Sponge grabs Submarine.)* Right through me! It was everywhere!

SUBMARINE: Keep it together.

SPONGE: I feel so...I can't describe it.

WASHCLOTH: *(Plaintive:)* Hold me.

SPONGE: I'm bloated. Heavy. Like—like I'll never be me again.

SUBMARINE: I thought I was going to pass out. I mean—he just kept holding me under the—whatever it was. Holding me, and pushing me around going "Awhoooga! Awhoooga!" *(Beat.)* What in the bathtub is an awhooga? Do you have any idea? You?

   (The others shake their heads.)

SUBMARINE: I kept thinking—he wants something. If I tell him, he'll let me breathe again. I was desperate—ask me a question—tell me what you want me to do, I'll do it! Whatever it is—I'll do it. He never asked any questions. Just kept saying...awhooga.

SPONGE: Awhooga?

RUBBER DUCKIE: Awhooga...

WASHCLOTH: Hold me.

SUBMARINE: Can he do that? Can he just do that to us?

RUBBER DUCKIE: Apparently.

SUBMARINE: We just...we have no rights?

RUBBER DUCKIE: How did you do it?

SUBMARINE: Do what?

RUBBER DUCKIE: Go under like that.

SUBMARINE: I don't—I just did.

RUBBER DUCKIE: I could never do that.

SUBMARINE: You wouldn't have had a choice. He drags you down there...awhooga!

RUBBER DUCKIE: I'd make a break for the surface, the first chance I'd get.

SUBMARINE: You say that now...

RUBBER DUCKIE: I don't get it—you guys—all three of you—just went under. I mean, Sponge stuck around for a while—

SPONGE: I held on as long as I could.

RUBBER DUCKIE: I know you did.

SPONGE: I just started feeling...heavy. This warm feeling, spreading up through me. And I sank, slowly, into oblivion.

SUBMARINE: Heavy.

SPONGE: Then...a resurrection—yanked upwards by an almighty hand, squeezed—squeezed to my very core. Then rubbed all over that dirty, sticky kid. What did I do to deserve that?

SUBMARINE: Awhooga...

WASHCLOTH: You sinned.

SPONGE: What?

WASHCLOTH: You're a sinner.

SPONGE: I'm a sponge!

WASHCLOTH: To be a sponge is to be a sinner.

SUBMARINE: So you're saying we brought this on ourselves, is that it? You're saying that I'm...awhooga?

WASHCLOTH: We are all awhooga.

SUBMARINE: Go soak your head.

(Washcloth goes and sulks in a corner.)

RUBBER DUCKIE: I didn't sink.

SUBMARINE: We noticed. You looked very happy, bobbing about. No worries for you — you took to that stuff like a...well...like a something to something, anyway.

RUBBER DUCKIE: Does that mean that I'm not awhooga?

SUBMARINE: You think you're better than us?

RUBBER DUCKIE: I'm not saying that.

SUBMARINE: Floating about —

SPONGE: Bet he never got squeezed by the hand.

RUBBER DUCKIE: I'm not saying I'm better than you — I'm just saying, perhaps, if you were more duck-like, you wouldn't have so much awhooga. Or be so awhooga... Or suffer from the awhoogas.

SPONGE: I'm duck-like.

SUBMARINE: You are not.

SPONGE: I'm more duck-like than you are.

SUBMARINE: Oh my goodness—you're a square blob! Does the duck have sharp corners? No. He's smooth—sleek. Very like, oh...a submarine, maybe?

SPONGE: You?

SUBMARINE: I think I have certain duck-like features.

SPONGE: I'm yellow!

SUBMARINE: What are you saying?

SPONGE: I'm not saying—I'm not saying! But I am yellow. Duck is yellow. You are gray. You've always been gray. You are always going to be gray.

SUBMARINE: I could be yellow if I wanted to be.

SPONGE: Submarines are gray.

SUBMARINE: There could be a yellow submarine.

SPONGE: Don't be ridiculous.

SUBMARINE: It's all about color with you, isn't it.

SPONGE: I can prove it.

SUBMARINE: You can't possibly prove—

SPONGE: Who sank first?

SUBMARINE: What?

SPONGE: Who. Sank. First.

(A moment.)

SUBMARINE: We all sank. I mean, we all—okay, except for the duck—but we all...

SPONGE: *We* all floated.

SUBMARINE: At first.

SPONGE: At first. Rubber Duckie stayed on top, he floats—

RUBBER DUCKIE: I have natural duckness. It's a gift.

SPONGE: Washcloth went gently, but only just below the surface. I mean, even after we'd been there forever, washcloth—she danced. Just below the surface, peeking her head out...

SUBMARINE: She got twisted up and poked in his ears!

SPONGE: But she was anointed with soap. She was cleansed. *(Beat.)* You sank.

SUBMARINE: I—

SPONGE: You sank.

SUBMARINE: The voice...

SPONGE: The voice spoke to you. Are we awhooga?

(A moment.)

SUBMARINE: It's me. I sank to the bottom. I was judged and found...awhooga.

(Submarine gets up and starts to walk away.)

RUBBER DUCKIE: Wait—

SUBMARINE: *(Distraught:)* I brought this on us. And I don't even know how.

(Submarine goes to Washcloth.)

SUBMARINE: Washcloth?

WASHCLOTH: Yes?

SUBMARINE: How do I find soap?

WASHCLOTH: Soap?

SUBMARINE: You were anointed with soap. You were cleansed. Will I get soap?

WASHCLOTH: A submarine doesn't get soap.

SUBMARINE: Why not?

(Washcloth shrugs. Submarine's almost in tears.)

He tried to drown me — and I don't know why. Perhaps...if I were more duck-like...

WASHCLOTH: You are who you are.

SUBMARINE: You get soap, I get drowned, Sponge gets squeezed...and Rubber Duckie rides above us all.

WASHCLOTH: Rubber Duckie got squeezed.

SUBMARINE: What?

WASHCLOTH: He got squeezed more than anyone. I heard him.

SUBMARINE: How could you hear —

WASHCLOTH: He squeaked. Whee-wheee!

SUBMARINE: No.

WASHCLOTH: Yes. Whee-whee!

SUBMARINE: That hypocrite!

(Submarine takes Washcloth's hand, and they go back to the others.)

SPONGE: Oh look — it's the sinking sinner and the soapy saint joining forces. Come to cleanse us of our awhooga?

SUBMARINE: *(To Rubber Duckie:)* You were squeezed.

Bath Time is Fun Time 11

SPONGE: Rubber Duckie was not squeezed! I was squeezed by the almighty hand, and I felt—lighter! As though the weight of the world was pouring out of me!

SUBMARINE: Duckie was squeezed. He squeaked!

RUBBER DUCKIE: I never squeak.

SUBMARINE: Washcloth heard you!

RUBBER DUCKIE: Washcloth lies.

(*Gasps.*)

WASHCLOTH: I don't lie.

RUBBER DUCKIE: You're lying right now. (*To Sponge:*) Who are you going to believe? A washcloth that sank in the first minute, or this...this submarine, who plunges to the very depths of the bathtub the moment he's placed in it. The *originator* of awhooga.

WASHCLOTH: I heard you.

SPONGE: We don't talk to people like you.

RUBBER DUCKIE: You said it, Sponge—let us away.

SUBMARINE: You think you're better than us.

RUBBER DUCKIE: I float above you.

WASHCLOTH: Forget it. It's no use.

SUBMARINE: He lies!

WASHCLOTH: It's not worth it.

SPONGE: Better listen to drip-dry there, sinker.

SUBMARINE: He squeaks!

SPONGE: He does not!

RUBBER DUCKIE: Never!

(Submarine darts forwards, grabs Duckie and SQUEEZES.)

Whee-whee!

(Sponge stares at Duckie in shocked horror.)

SPONGE: You...You just...

(A moment.)

RUBBER DUCKIE: Okay, so I got squeezed!

SPONGE: You got squeezed.

RUBBER DUCKIE: And I squeaked. It was all I could do not to throw up.

SUBMARINE: Why didn't you tell us?

SPONGE: You lied to me.

RUBBER DUCKIE: I...I just felt so...I was just...bobbing about. I kept bobbing, up and down and up and down. I started feeling sick. And then...then he started splashing. *(Beat.)* I was adrift. I couldn't hang on to the side, I couldn't do anything...just tossed to and fro, bobbing...bobbing. Completely out of my control. I tipped over. *(Beat.)* I don't know what we did. Maybe, we're born in a state of awhooga, maybe we...maybe there are no answers. Some of us sink, some of us float. We're soaped and squeezed, rubbed, poked into ears...

WASHCLOTH: Ears? I *wish* it was only his ears.

RUBBER DUCKIE: We bob—adrift. We sink, alone. There are no answers. If he's awhooga, maybe we all are. But eventually, the plug was pulled and that terrible— whatever—spiralled away. And we try to take stock, to put our lives back together. To look at ourselves in the distorted reflection of the spout and say...thank you. It is over, and we'll never—never ever—have to go through that again.

SUBMARINE: Amen.

SPONGE: Amen.

WASHCLOTH: Hold me.

(They hug.)

(Lights fade out. End of play.)

The Author Speaks

What inspired you to write this play?
I wrote this play for an evening of one acts called *Makin' a Splash* from the North Dakota theatre company Youth Education on Stage. They asked for submissions of plays set in or next to water. I assumed most of the writers would choose the beach or a lakeside for their entries, and I wanted to stand out. I started with the idea of writing a play that takes place next to a bathtub, and everything flowed from that choice.

Was the structure or other elements of the play influenced by any other work?
I don't think so. There aren't many bath-toy-centric works that come to mind, at least.

Have you dealt with the same theme in other works that you have written?
I have—in many of my more adult dramas. This is most certainly a wacky, "bath toys afraid of water" humorous script—but it is also a painful drama dealing with guilt, with loss in the face of trauma. This is a script about a soldier coming back from serving in Iraq and feeling, as he described it, that he had "lost the part of himself that allowed him to talk to God." This is a piece about losing one's faith and finding one's humanity, and when I wrote Submarine's line "I brought this on us. And I don't even know how," I was weeping. Seriously, I was trying to type that line while I was crying so much that I couldn't see the keyboard. So yes, it's a wacky comedy about bath toys, and yes, I'm probably too emotional and should learn to rein in my mawkishness—or at least learn to touch-type—but there is more depth to this piece than you might imagine at

first glance.

What writers have had the most profound effect on your style?
In each of my playwright questionnaires (YouthPLAYS has published seven of my plays so far), I've tried to mention a different influence on my writing. This time around, I think I'll throw a shout out to Terry Pratchett, my favorite fiction author. There's a depth of philosophy to even his most humorous, light-hearted work that makes it so much more than mere fantasy. I'd like to hope, in some small way, *Bath Time is Fun Time* aspires to have that wonderful dichotomy of the ridiculous conveying the sublime.

What do you hope to achieve with this work?
I would like to start a massive online petition to free bath toys everywhere from their oppression. Okay, not really. I'd be happy with making a few people laugh.

What were the biggest challenges involved in the writing of this play?
The voice of the Rubber Duckie—every now and then, he'd start sounding like Krusty the Clown (from The Simpsons) in my head, and then they would all start talking like that. Try Washcloth's line: "Ears. I wish it was only his ears," in the voice of Krusty, and you'll see what I mean. I had to fight against it, and please try not to do it in performance, of course—unless you are in fact Dan Castellaneta, the voice of Krusty, in which case go ahead—and can I please have your autograph?

What are the most common mistakes that occur in productions of your work?
I use a fairly standard set of punctuation to indicate the end

of a partial line: an em-dash for an interruption and an ellipsis for a character trailing off. There's a lot of difference between a character being stopped from saying what they were going to; or a character making an active choice not to verbalize something they were going to say. In either case, part of your character work as an actor is to figure out—from the clues in the text—what the character would have said. It matters.

What inspired you to become a playwright?
My first production, at the Summer Shorts Festival at the Miami City Theatre. I saw a notice online that they were accepting ten-minute plays. I'd been writing for years, but I'd never even considered writing a play. I saw the notice and thought "Ten minutes? I could write a ten-minute play." I did, it was accepted from over 850 submissions, and a couple of months later, I was watching my first ever play on stage in front of an audience of 300, sandwiched in between Paul Rudnick's *Pride and Joy* and Colin Mitchell's *The Leap*. Feeling the audience response all around me clarified what I wanted to do in my writing and in my life, and I've been writing plays ever since.

How did you research the subject?
I had many, many bath toys as a child. My favorite was a submarine that dove and resurfaced when you squeezed a plastic bulb connected to it by tubing. I guess that counts as research, right?

Are any characters modeled after real life or historical figures?
Yes, they are carefully modeled after four famous philosophers: Sartre, Camus, Hegel and I can't even think of a fourth, because I'm making this up completely. They're

just bath toys...wounded, broken bath toys who are also trauma survivors. I have so many friends who have survived trauma, from abuse in the home to the horrors of war. I didn't base these characters on any of them in particular, but on all of them, and so all of us. Is that sufficiently pretentious? I'm trying, here. Bath toys, remember? One of them's a rubber duck, for Pete's sake.

Do any films/videos exist of prior productions of this play?
There are a couple of versions out there—including a production by the Unsaddest Factory Theatre Company with some wonderfully elaborate costumes. It's easily found on YouTube.

Shakespeare gave advice to the players in Hamlet; if you could give advice to your cast what would it be?
Don't play these as cartoon characters—play them as real people, honestly suffering from deep trauma. The more seriously you play the characters, the funnier the situation gets. The moment you start playing them "wacky," the magic goes out of the scene. Find the humanity, try your best to make the audience cry, and they will laugh even harder.

How was the first production different from the vision that you created in your mind?
I was unfortunately unable to see the premiere—but there's a photo of it on my website, arthurjolly.com, and it looks much like I imagined—except that they seem so young. I wrote this for adult actors as much as for youth theatre, and I've since seen it performed by 60 year olds, to great effect. It's a wonderfully universal piece of theatre—bath toys can be any age, any gender, any race, any ability.

Can I contact the playwright?
Yes! I'm on Facebook, or at www.arthurjolly.com. I'm happy to answer emails from directors, actors or theatres working on my plays or considering them. I love being part of the rehearsal process, and I frequently arrange my travel plans to attend productions, make classroom appearances, teach workshops, meet with theatre companies, or have audience talkbacks. Writing can be a solitary profession, and while the voices in my head sometimes sound like Krusty the Clown, they don't really substitute for actual human interaction.

About the Author

Arthur M. Jolly was recognized by the Academy of Motion Picture Arts and Sciences with a Nicholl Fellowship in Screenwriting, and is the playwright of more than 50 produced plays, including *A Gulag Mouse* (Finalist Woodward/Newman Drama Award, Winner Off-Broadway Competition, Joining Sword and Pen Competition), *Past Curfew* (AOPW Fellowship winner), *Trash* (Joining Sword and Pen Competition, Semi-Finalist Eugene O'Neill Conference), *A Very Modern Marriage* (Semi-Finalist Eugene O'Neill Conference) and a collection of ten-minute plays *Guilty Moments*. His plays published by YouthPLAYS include *Long Joan Silver, What the Well Dressed Girl is Wearing, Snakes in a Lunchbox, How Blue is My Crocodile, Moby (No Last Name Given)* and *The Christmas Princess*. Jolly is represented by the Brant Rose Agency. Upcoming productions at www.arthurjolly.com.

About YouthPLAYS

YouthPLAYS (www.youthplays.com) is a publisher of award-winning professional dramatists and talented new discoveries, each with an original theatrical voice, and all dedicated to expanding the vocabulary of theatre for young actors and audiences. On our website you'll find one-act and full-length plays and musicals for teen and pre-teen (and even college) actors, as well as duets and monologues for competition. Many of our authors' works have been widely produced at high schools and middle schools, youth theatres and other TYA companies, both amateur and professional, as well as at elementary schools, camps, churches and other institutions serving young audiences and/or actors worldwide. Most are intended for performance by young people, while some are intended for adult actors performing for young audiences.

YouthPLAYS was co-founded by professional playwrights Jonathan Dorf and Ed Shockley. It began merely as an additional outlet to market their own works, which included a substantial body of award-winning published and unpublished plays and musicals. Those interested in their published plays were directed to the respective publishers' websites, and unpublished plays were made available in electronic form. But when they saw the desperate need for material for young actors and audiences – coupled with their experience that numerous quality plays for young people weren't finding a home – they made the decision to represent the work of other playwrights as well. Dozens and dozens of authors are now members of the YouthPLAYS family, with scripts available both electronically and in traditional acting editions. We continue to grow as we look for exciting and challenging plays and musicals for young actors and audiences.

About ProduceaPlay.com

Let's put up a play! Great idea! But producing a play takes time, energy and knowledge. While finding the necessary time and energy is up to you, ProduceaPlay.com is a website designed to assist you with that third element: knowledge.

Created by YouthPLAYS' co-founders, Jonathan Dorf and Ed Shockley, ProduceaPlay.com serves as a resource for producers at all levels as it addresses the many facets of production. As Dorf and Shockley speak from their years of experience (as playwrights, producers, directors and more), they are joined by a group of award-winning theatre professionals and experienced teachers from the world of academic theatre, all making their expertise available for free in the hope of helping this and future generations of producers, whether it's at the school or university level, or in community or professional theatres.

The site is organized into a series of major topics, each of which has its own page that delves into the subject in detail, offering suggestions and links for further information. For example, Publicity covers everything from Publicizing Auditions to How to Use Social Media to Posters to whether it's worth hiring a publicist. Casting details Where to Find the Actors, How to Evaluate a Resume, Callbacks and even Dealing with Problem Actors. You'll find guidance on your Production Timeline, The Theater Space, Picking a Play, Budget, Contracts, Rehearsing the Play, The Program, House Management, Backstage, and many other important subjects.

The site is constantly under construction, so visit often for the latest insights on play producing, and let it help make your play production dreams a reality.

From the YouthPLAYS Blog: *The Vanishing Monologue, II*

Many decades ago, while working with master teacher Marsha Pincus at Gratz High School, we introduced the "collaborative emotive monologue" exercise as a tool to quickly teach the concept of movement in dialogue.

The idea for the exercise had its origins in a workshop conducted when I worked as a bank teller in Manhattan's busy garment district. The seminar goal was to teach how to move clients along more quickly without offense and to help diffuse the resentment inspired by the long lines in those pre-computer days of commerce.

The workshop facilitator described the scenario of a man who has just been released from his job without severance. He gets caught in the rain en route to a tepid cup of fast food coffee and encounters a super perky cheerleader. In most cases, her ebullient mood makes him want to slap her.

The speaker continued on to explain that emotions are organized along a continuum and that we interact best when someone is at or near our current emotional state. More importantly he asserted that we can "walk" someone up or down this emotional scale.

CHARACTER A: I hate Friday afternoons!

CHARACTER B: You got that right.

CHARACTER A: But at least the week's almost over.

CHARACTER B: One more hour.

CHARACTER A: Then it's party time.

CHARACTER B: Pizza and martinis!

CHARACTER A: Plus it's Super Bowl weekend, right?

CHARACTER B: I forgot. Man, this is my favorite weekend of the whole year!!

While I cannot attest definitively to the science of this theory, a lifetime of play crafting has convinced me beyond any doubt that this device is a useful tool with which to construct dialogue. It connects one idea to the next and makes it easier for an actor to access the emotions required for a scene.

This incremental and logical advance of emotion is even more useful to an actor when he is performing a monologue. The march from one clear emotion to the next means that an actor need not struggle to manufacture feelings while he is alone onstage or interacting with a silent partner. It also creates the feeling of perpetual movement that is essential when a single actor is attempting to hold the attention of an audience.

Rather than a primal scream...

    "I'm angry, I'm angry, I'm angry..."

a monologue constructed with knowledge of the tone scale becomes dynamic...

    "I'm ticked off. I'm angry. I'm livid. I'm overwhelmed. I'm spent. I'm apathetic."

and inspires an author to find novel ways to express each emotion:

    HURT - I can't believe he'd do that; not with her.

    FEAR - If it's true then it means he never loved me.

    RAGE - I deserve better from both of them.

    DESPAIR - And now Mom can say, "I told you so," again.

    REGRET - I never should have let him into my heart.

Wait—there's more! Read this and other blog entries in their entirety at www.youthplays.com.

More from YouthPLAYS

Long Joan Silver by Arthur M. Jolly
Comedy. 90-100 minutes. 6-15 males, 8-20 females (14-30 performers possible, plus extras).

The classic adventure tale of buried treasure—and the original one-legged pirate with a parrot—gets a timely makeover, combining offbeat farce, sight gags and horrendous puns with a dramatic core that explores discrimination, privilege and greed. Unlike in Robert Louis Stevenson's book, where only one unnamed character is female, women are front and center as ***Long Joan Silver***'s young Jim Hawkins comes of age during the fateful voyage of the Hispaniola and the clash between an all-female pirate crew and Squire Trelawney, Doctor Livesey and the domineering Captain Smollett.

Of Love and Shampoo by Jonathan Josephson
Comedy. 30-35 minutes. 2 males, 2 females.

Life is pretty awful when you've accidentally locked yourself in the bathroom, especially on the night you're supposed to meet your girlfriend's parents. A madcap comedy about four friends, one very important date, and the locked door that brings them together.

The Locker Next 2 Mine by Jonathan Dorf
Dramedy. 80-85 minutes. 5-12+ males, 8-16+ females (14-40 performers possible).

Alisa arrives at a new high school in the middle of the year to find her locker next to a shrine for a popular lacrosse player who's died in an auto accident, but as she digs deeper, she discovers another death that no one talks about, even as it's left many of the school's students trying to pick up their own pieces. A play about teen suicide and dealing with loss.

Jennifer the Unspecial: Time Travel, Love Potions & 8th Grade by Matthew Mezzacappa (book & lyrics) & Cynthia Chi-Wing Wong (music)
Musical. 90 minutes. 5-30 males, 3-30 females (8-60 performers possible).

When her science teacher's invention goes horribly wrong, awkward, clumsy eighth grader Jennifer finds herself thrust into a time-traveling adventure with three of her classmates. Through the journey, as they encounter warriors, artists, presidents and love potions, Jennifer discovers she doesn't need anyone's approval to be absolutely amazing and special.

Lipstick and Heroics by Evan Baughfman
Comedy. 50-60 minutes. 6 females.

Superheroine group A.W.S.U.M. (Amazing Women Saving Untold Millions) searches for new members after eighty percent of the original team is killed in an attack by villainess Suprema. Five unique young women attend the tryout, each ready to compete for a spot in the group, but a shocking plot is afoot (well, shocking for a comedy!): one of the recruits is actually a spy for Suprema, sent to kill the others and put an end to A.W.S.U.M. once and for all...

Choose Your Own Oz by Tommy Jamerson
Comedy. 85-100 minutes. 4-15+ females, 4-15+ males (10-30+ performers possible).

The Wizard of Oz meets *Choose Your Own Adventure* in this fresh and fast-paced retelling of the L. Frank Baum classic in which the audience plays playwright and gets the chance to change everything from Dorothy's footwear (silver slippers or ruby red...clown shoes?) to Toto's species (lion, tiger or octopus?—oh my!). A delight for children of all ages, ***Choose Your Own Oz*** reminds us all that at the end of the day, there really is no place like home.

Made in the USA
Charleston, SC
05 January 2017